BC

Written by Christelle Legros

Translated by Rebecca Neal

Tristan
and Isolde

BY RENÉ LOUIS

Bright
≡Summaries.com

RENÉ LOUIS

FRENCH HISTORIAN, PHILOLOGIST AND ARCHAEOLOGIST

- **Born in Yonne (France) in 1906**
- **Died in 1991**
- **His work:**
  - *Tristan and Isolde* (1972), novel

The historian, philologist and archaeologist René Louis taught medieval literary history in various universities between 1941 and 1977. In 1927 he discovered the Carolingian frescoes in the crypts at Saint-Germain (Auxerre), which made his reputation as a medievalist. A pupil of Joseph Bédier and Ferdinand Lot, his publications are milestones in the world of academia.

TRISTAN AND ISOLDE

CHARACTERS LED INTO MADNESS BY THEIR ALL-CONSUMING LOVE

- **Genre:** novel
- **Reference edition:** Louis, R. (1972) *Tristan et Iseult*. Paris: Librairie Générale Française.[1]
- **First edition:** 1972
- **Themes:** love, madness, potions, magic, drama, jealousy, betrayal

The legend of Tristan and Isolde is of Celtic origin. There are remarkable written traces of it in French medieval literature from the 12th century onwards, mainly in the form of fragments. Since then, multiple versions of the legend have been published, including that of René Louis. Although Louis's text has not yet been translated into English, this summary will use the anglicised names of the legend's characters to aid understanding.

This legend depicts a trio that is famous in literary history: the husband (King Mark), his wife (Queen Isolde the Fair) and her lover (Tristan). The story makes use of many elements of the Celtic source, including magic. In this way, drinking a magic potion awakens the passionate love that brings together Tristan and Isolde and transcends all human and divine laws.

---

1. All quotations taken from the reference edition have been translated by BrightSummaries.com

SUMMARY

While paying tribute to Joseph Bédier (French critic, 1864-1938), who renewed the legend of Tristan and Isolde at the start of the 20th century, René Louis stated that he wanted to use the same sources to recreate a kind of tale which predates feudal and chivalric civilisation, going back to the High Middle Ages in Celtic Great Britain. His aim was to produce a version that was closer to the early legend of Tristan, differing in this way from those of Bédier and the authors of the 12th century.

THE IRISH GIANT

One day an Irish giant, Morholt, threatens to claim a tribute from King Mark, who reigns over Cornwall. None of the barons dare to challenge him, apart from Tristan, who then reveals his identity: he is in fact King Mark's nephew, the son of the monarch's younger sister Blancheflor and Rivalen, the son of the King of Lyonesse. Educated by a squire named Gorvenal from the age of seven, when his father died he came to his uncle's court under a false name so as to gain recognition for his bravery.

Although he wins the fight, Tristan is injured by a poisoned spear. Unable to be cured, he leaves on a boat and washes up in Ireland, where he is cared for by Queen Isolde and her daughter, Isolde the Fair. When he is finally cured, he returns to Cornwall. The treacherous barons are jealous of Tristan and accuse him of trying to become his uncle's successor by stopping him from marrying and producing an heir. King

Mark ends up choosing as his wife the woman whose hair, fair as gold, was brought by the swallows. Recognising young Isolde's hair, Tristan sets off to win her for his uncle.

THE DRAGON

Gormond, the King of Ireland, promises Isolde to whoever will free the country of the dragon which plagues it. Tristan kills the monster and takes its tongue as a trophy, but when he touches the tongue he is poisoned. The king's chief steward, who saw this scene, cuts off the dragon's head and proclaims himself champion. But Isolde refuses to marry him, convinced that the true victor is concealed nearby. She and her mother find Tristan and care for him again. When she sees that a shard found in the head of her Uncle Morholt comes from Tristan's sword, Isolde becomes angry and wants to kill him, but the young man manages to reason with her by promising to defend her against the steward.

It is realised that Tristan killed the monster: he is therefore the one who should marry Isolde. Gormond, to whom he reveals his true intentions, agrees to give his daughter to King Mark. Meanwhile, the queen prepares a special "wine" which can awaken passion in the man and woman who drink it. She gives it to Isolde's servant Brangaine, so that she can give an equal serving to Mark and Isolde on their wedding night. She does not suspect that it will be Tristan, not Mark, who drinks the potion.

THE LOVE POTION

As they are crossing the sea, Brangaine reassures Isolde that her marriage will be happy by telling her about the magic potion. However, the girl refuses to share the wine with Mark and the servant, surmising that Isolde is in love with Tristan, decides to make them drink the potion. It takes effect immediately: as they are overcome by love, they surrender to carnal passion. To hide this from Mark, Isolde asks Brangaine, who is a virgin, to take her place in the king's bed on their wedding night. Mark falls for the trick, which allows the satisfied Isolde to continue her relationship with Tristan.

However, the carefree lovers gradually put themselves in danger. When Kariado, a faithful follower of Mark, catches them, he is jealous and warns the king, who decides to test the queen. Isolde gets out of the situation thanks to Brangaine, before being won over by a tune that a baron of Ireland plays on the harp. Tristan uses another crafty trick to free her. Next, the barons catch the two lovers and inform the king, who banishes Tristan. He then hides in the forest so as to remain close to Isolde: like hazel and honeysuckle, the lovers cannot live apart from one another without risking death.

A DEADLY TRAP

The king is informed by Frocin the dwarf that Tristan and Isolde have been meeting at night in the orchard, close to the fountain, and decides to surprise them by hiding in a pine tree in the orchard. However, Tristan sees his reflection in the fountain and changes his manner when the queen approaches. She becomes suspicious and talks in a way that exonerates her lover. The unsuspecting Mark trusts his nephew and invites him back to court. Proud of their trick, Tristan and Isolde are unaware that they will soon be sentenced to death.

The treacherous barons still want to catch the lovers in the act, and ask Frocin to spread flour on the floor between the beds of Tristan and the queen. When he discovers this trap, Tristan jumps into Isolde's bed, but in doing so he injures himself. The bloodstains are a sure sign of the lovers' guilt: driven mad with rage, the king decides to have them put to death without a trial.

THE LOVERS' FLIGHT

On his way to the stake, Tristan asks to stop so that he can pray in a chapel overhanging a cliff. He throws himself off the cliff, lands without injuring himself, and runs away. The king is furious and demands that Isolde be publicly burned right away. There is a band of lepers in the crowd, and their leader suggests to the king that he give Isolde to them: that way, her punishment will be worse than death. The king accepts this offer, but Tristan and Gorvenal attack the lepers and free the queen.

Having taken shelter in the forest of Morois, the lovers lead a difficult life full of hardship, which painfully weakens them. They meet a hermit, Brother Ogrin, who encourages them to repent. However, it is "not in their power to renounce their love" (p. 119). One night, they fall asleep with Tristan's sword between them. A forester sees them and tells the king, who is moved by the sight of them sleeping so chastely and demonstrates his clemency by letting them sleep.

ISOLDE'S TRIAL

Three years after taking the potion, the spell has worn off, but both Tristan and Isolde feel that their love remains. Nonetheless, for their own good they must return to a normal life. The hermit agrees to help them by writing a letter to Mark. The king replies that he accepts Isolde's return, but not Tristan's. The lovers promise to always help each other and, as a token of this oath, Tristan offers Isolde his dog, and she gives him her magic ring. Isolde is given a fine welcome by the king, while Tristan goes to hide so that he can receive news of the queen.

The treacherous barons call for her to be put on trial. Isolde agrees to justify herself in order to eliminate any suspicion. However, it is important to her not to lie before God and, with the help of Brangaine, she comes up with a plan. Since the oath will be sworn at Mal Pas, the plan involves asking a leper, who is really Tristan in disguise, to help her cross the ford. Isolde sits astride Tristan; then when she testifies, she swears before God that "no man other than her husband, King Mark, and this leper have ever been between her legs" (p. 156).

In this way, Isolde's innocence is proven. However, Mark is not eager to summon Tristan back to him. The latter wants to leave the country, but is prevented from doing so by his love for Isolde. He therefore comes back to find her risking death, but she is aware of the danger and begs him to flee.

TRISTAN'S EXILE

On his way, Tristan meets some Knights of the Round Table and accompanies them to court in order to see Isolde before his exile. The king lets the group stay in his bedroom, but has scythes put on the floor because he does not trust them. When he joins Isolde, Tristan injures himself again. Luckily, he is saved by Keu, the seneschal (an officer in charge of administrative and domestic arrangements in noble houses during the Middle Ages), who has the hunters get up so that the entire room is covered in blood and Tristan is not caught. Finally, he sets off for Brittany with Gorvenal.

Once they have arrived, they take shelter with King Hoel of Brittany, the father of Sir Kahedin and Isolde of the White Hands. By marrying the other Isolde, whose beauty and name remind him of his former lover, Tristan tries in vain to console himself. When Kariado slyly tells Isolde the Fair about Tristan's marriage, the queen, who has not forgotten him and is in great distress, sings a lay announcing death.

ISOLDE OF THE WHITE HANDS

While Tristan and Isolde of the White Hands are out walking, water from the ford splashes the young bride, who exclaims that the water is bolder than her husband. Indeed, in spite of the young woman's beauty, their union has not been consummated. Kahedin is angered by this but, once Tristan tells him everything, he forgives his friend and suggests that he return to England in order to make sure of the love of Isolde the Fair.

On his return to Cornwall, Tristan hides in order to see the queen again. When he imitates the song of a bird, she recognises him and, thanks to Brangaine, the lovers meet again. But one day, her pride wounded by a misunderstanding, Isolde refuses to recognise Tristan and has him chased away. He despairs for a year, then, determined to see her again, he crosses the sea again and pretends to be mad. Thanks to Brangaine and Tristan's dog Husdent, the lovers meet each other. Isolde apologises and swears that she will never stop loving Tristan, who then leaves again.

Sinking into melancholy, he builds a palace of pictures, where he erects sculptures in honour of Isolde the Fair and their love.

THE BLACK SAIL

Poisoned by a lance, Tristan asks Kahedin to go find Isolde the Fair, the only person who can cure him, and fights to stay alive, sustained by the hope of seeing her one last time. Kahedin agrees to this, and announces that he will carry two sails on his ship: a white sail, which will indicate the return of his beloved, and a black one, which will show that Isolde refuses to help him.

But Isolde of the White Hands, who has overheard everything, wants to take revenge, and when her brother returns she lies to Tristan and tells him that the sail is black. Tristan dies and Isolde the Fair, discovering the body of her beloved, collapses and also dies. Kahedin takes their bodies back to Cornwall, where they will be buried. Two bushes grow from their tombs, a hazel and a honeysuckle, which are impossible to separate.

CHARACTER STUDY

KING MARK

Mark reigns over Cornwall and hails from an ancient lineage. Having reached later life, he still has no wife and no heir. Noble, generous, loyal and courageous, he is nonetheless often short-tempered. His moods are unpredictable, and he can prove violent and cruel. He excels above all at hunting.

His authority over his vassals is shaky: as he is easily intimidated by his barons, he is influenced and manipulated by their words and schemes. He is also naïve and gullible, which means that he often puts his trust in appearances and takes them for reality. In this way, he grants the lovers his complete trust and clemency as soon as a kind or skilfully chosen word chases the darkest suspicions from his mind. This character trait makes him volatile: when he is seized by doubt, he is very angry; when he is pacified by what he sees or hears, he once again becomes merciful and freely forgives people.

Yet in spite of everything, King Mark tenderly loves his wife and Tristan. When he is forced to exile the latter, he is grieved by it. When he recovers the bodies of his wife and nephew, he honours them by burying them side by side instead of burning them. As such, in the end it is clemency that prevails in his heart.

TRISTAN

Born in Lyonesse, Tristan is the son of Blancheflor, King Mark's youngest sister, and Rivalen, the son of the King of Lyonesse. His father baptises him with the Celtic name "Drustan", which becomes "Tristan", a name which better signifies his parents' sadness at his birth and which foreshadows the trials and misfortunes he will later face (the French word *triste* means "sad"). Indeed, Blancheflor dies during childbirth and Rivalen, despairing, leaves him an orphan at the age of fifteen. From the age of seven, Tristan is raised by Gorvenal, who will always remain faithful to him, and his education is completed by Seneschal Dinas of Lidan after his arrival in Cornwall.

Tristan has the qualities of a true knight: he is handsome, gallant, courageous, faithful to his king and to his beloved, loyal, and valiant. His feats place him above all the barons. Tristan is gifted with great, almost superhuman, physical strength (think back to his victories against the giant and the dragon), and he is skilled in all the arts: he is an excellent poet, harpist, imitator of birdsong, courser, hunter and squire. He is also cunning (for example when he gets Isolde back from the Irish baron), makes ingenious tools (his bow, which he calls Fail-not) and knows the secrets of plants to change his appearance, conceal himself by taking on another identity, or disguise his voice.

However, the ingestion of the potion irrevocably alters his path, which seemed to be already laid out. Then Tristan experiences the torments of jealousy and has several brushes with death to see Isolde the Fair. Indeed, madness lies in wait for him when he spends too long apart from his beloved. Furthermore, his behaviour towards Isolde of the White Hands is unreasoning and unfair. This inspires jealousy in his young wife, ultimately leading to the deaths of the lovers.

ISOLDE THE FAIR

She is twelve years old when the injured Tristan arrives in the castle of her father, King Gormond of Ireland. While Tristan is recovering, she becomes his pupil: he teaches her music and singing. Her blonde hair shines like gold. She is courteous and possesses all the qualities that a man could wish for in a wife. She is a healer and knows the secrets of plants thanks to the teachings of her mother Queen Isolde, Morholt's sister.

Torn between her sense of duty towards her husband and her all-consuming passion for Tristan, Isolde uses every strategy available to her to maintain her two roles as married woman and lover. She does not want to give up either of them. She is very cunning and manages to get out of delicate situations with the help of her faithful servant Brangaine. She can also prove cruel, proud and merciless (notably in the episodes where she wants to have Brangaine killed and when she has Tristan chased away). But she realises her wrongs and punishes herself (for example by making herself wear a hair shirt). Isolde seems less innocent than Tristan from the moment when, having been informed by Brangaine about the power of the wine prepared by her mother, she lets Tristan drink it when he is thirsty. She then shares the cup with him and not with her husband as had initially been planned because, in her heart, she is attracted to him after his victory over the Irish dragon. After Tristan has left to go to Brittany, she is also tormented by jealousy and loneliness.

ISOLDE OF THE WHITE HANDS

The daughter of King Hoel of Brittany, Isolde of the White Hands is "beautiful and learned" (p. 168). Her resemblance to Isolde the Fair earns her Tristan's attention and interest, and in a moment of profound bitterness he asks her to marry him. Young and in love, she joyfully accepts. This news also delights her brother Sir Kahedin, who likes Tristan. However, on their wedding night Tristan cannot consummate the marriage because he sees Isolde the Fair's face reflected in the green jasper ring she gave him before their separation. Isolde of the White Hands, who is ignorant of such matters, does not take offence. She proves patient and tender with her husband, although one day she complains to Kahedin about her situation and she does suffer because of it. When she finds out the truth about the love which unites Tristan and Isolde the Fair, her resigned tenderness turns into a violent desire for revenge. The jealousy which brutally torments her awakens her malicious side; this is why she tells Tristan that the sail is black when it is really white. The death of Tristan, and then of Isolde, is her revenge.

BRANGAINE

Bought as a child from Norwegian pirates, Brangaine was

raised with Isolde the Fair and they are the same age. Even though Brangaine is Isolde's servant, she is also her playmate and her only confidant. Wise and shrewd, she is also cunning. She deliberately makes a mistake, thus betraying the trust of the Queen of Ireland, when she gives the wine to Tristan and Isolde. Nonetheless, this is done with the aim of helping her mistress, to whom she dedicates a deep love. She will remain faithful to her whatever happens. More than once, she helps her to find Tristan: she acts as lookout for the lovers, she takes the queen's place in the king's bed on their wedding night, she lies to Mark to protect Isolde, etc. She is often referred to as "dear Brangaine".

GORVENAL

The faithful Gorvenal is to Tristan what Brangaine is to Isolde the Fair. It is he, the wise squire, who educates Tristan and accompanies him in all his adventures, escapes and trials. As such, when the lovers are banished in the forest he helps them as much as he can by making baskets for them to pick food, and he does not hesitate to kill any enemies of Tristan that he meets on the road (the forester who comes across the lovers sleeping and betrays them, and one of the treacherous barons). But Gorvenal is wiser than his pupil. When Tristan seeks to see Isolde again at any price, Gorvenal warns him and tries to dissuade him from his overly risky plans. Gorvenal dies during a last expedition led by Sir Kahedin, the brother of Isolde of the White Hands.

ANALYSIS

ACTANCIAL MODEL

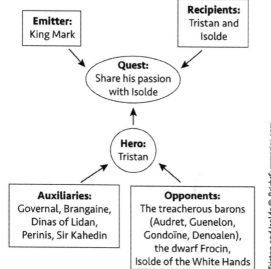

Emitter:
King Mark

Recipients:
Tristan and
Isolde

Quest:
Share his passion
with Isolde

Hero:
Tristan

Auxiliaries:
Governal, Brangaine,
Dinas of Lidan,
Perinis, Sir Kahedin

Opponents:
The treacherous barons
(Audret, Guenelon,
Gondoïne, Denoalen),
the dwarf Frocin,
Isolde of the White Hands

Tristan and Isolde © BrightSummaries.com

NARRATIVE OUTLINE

Tristan and Isolde is a narrative text, and therefore follows the classic narrative outline. It tells of the passion which unites Tristan and Isolde and which defies all human and divine laws.

Initial situation: this is the beginning of the story, the moment where the author sets the scene and introduces the characters; the situation is stable, which means that it has no reason to develop.

- King Mark reigns over Cornwall, surrounded by his vassals and his barons. His nephew Tristan's exceptional qualities make him the worthiest of his defenders.

Disruptive element: this is an event which disturbs the initial situation and triggers the beginning of the story.

- The king's barons demand that he take a wife in order to produce an heir. Tristan leaves for Ireland in search of the only woman the king will consent to marry: Isolde the Fair. On their way back, however, Isolde and Tristan drink the love potion meant for Isolde and Mark, and are joined by an unbreakable love. Tristan becomes the king's rival.

Developments: these are the events caused by the disruptive element and which bring about the action(s) undertaken by the protagonist to resolve the problem. There are two major developments in the story:

- When the potion takes effect. Tristan and Isolde are so in love that they are careless, but every time they are saved at the very last moment, up until the day when they are caught. When they are condemned, they flee and take shelter in the forest, where they live in poverty. Nonetheless, the potion spares them from physical and emotional suffering: they are together, and that is all that matters.

- When the potion wears off. The lovers are no longer under the magical protection of the wine. They then feel all the pain of the existence they are leading and become worried about their fate: it is time for them to separate. They still love each other, but with a human love; from that moment on they experience the anguish, doubts and torments of their passion. Isolde returns to the king and the couple that was initially planned are back together. However, Tristan and Isolde pine for each other, which causes Tristan to return to the queen repeatedly.

Outcome: this puts an end to the developments and leads to the conclusion.

- During a last adventure, Tristan is injured and poisoned for the third time. Nobody can treat him, except Isolde the Fair. At the same time, Isolde of the White Hands learns the truth about her husband's past. She is jealous, and now her only desire is to take revenge. She therefore lies to Tristan, which leads to his death.

Conclusion: this is the end of the story. The situation is once again stable, like the initial situation, but transformations have taken place.

- Isolde the Fair dies of despair over her lover's body. Their bodies are sent back to Cornwall to King Mark, who forgives them and buries them side by side. The lovers are eternally reunited in death. The two shrubs which grow from their tombs and intertwine their branches symbolise this unbreakable love.

A NOVEL WHICH BORDERS ON THE MAGICAL

Tristan and Isolde, which, like all legends, first circulated orally, was then written down in a Romance language, a precursor to modern French which coexisted with Latin during the Middle Ages. In contrast to Latin, this language was considered a vulgar language. This is why the story of Tristan and Isolde is described as a *roman* (French for "novel"). Nonetheless, the legend of the two lovers exists in many forms: lays (the lay is a short narrative form, a sort of short story in verse, that was popular during the 12th and 13th centuries), long narrative poems in verse (specifically in octosyllables, meaning in lines containing eight syllables), and novels in prose. There are, in addition, two differing versions: an epic version which juxtaposes sequences written in a coarse style with no transitions, which is poorly suited to psychological analysis; and a lyric version, which contains numerous dramatic monologues and develops the love of the two main characters. The most famous example of the epic version is the one by Béroul (Anglo-Norman troubadour, 12th century), while the most famous lyric version is by Thomas of Britain (Anglo-Norman troubadour, 12th century), who presents a courtly, chivalric version.

The presence of magical elements in the story (the love potion, the dragon, the giant, the magic ring etc.) may also bring to mind the tale form, as may the fact that certain scenes are repeated: Tristan is twice injured, poisoned and then cured by Isolde the Fair and her mother; Tristan's successive disguises, where he is recognised by Isolde and Brangaine, etc.

Finally, it is worth explaining that, before being written down, the legend was circulated by storytellers who saw the magical obligation represented by the potion as an alibi for the lovers and a way of inviting the audience to sympathise with the protagonists' suffering and to forgive them. It was also an opportunity to think about the place of love in feudal society: should people advocate a love that goes against all laws, or should they take the side of the established order and marriage? The written reworkings of the legend vary between these two options.

We want to hear from you!
Leave a comment on your online library
and share your favourite books on social media!

FURTHER READING

REFERENCE EDITION

- Louis, R. (1972) *Tristan et Iseult*. Paris: Librairie Générale Française.

REFERENCE STUDIES

- Baumgartner, E. (1993) Les romans de Tristan et Iseut. *Patrimoine littéraire européen. Le Moyen Âge, de l'Oural à l'Atlantique. Littératures d'Europe occidentale.* Brussels: De Boeck University, pp. 489-501.
- De Beaumarchais, J.-P. and Rey, A. (1984) *Dictionnaire des littératures de langue française*. Paris: Bordas, pp. 2333-2338.
- Laffont, R. and Bompiani, V. (1960). *Dictionnaire des personnages littéraires et dramatiques de tous les temps et de tous les pays*. Paris: Robert Laffont, pp. 506-507 and pp. 967-968.
- Laffont, R. and Bompiani, V. (1994) *Le Nouveau Dictionnaire des oeuvres de tous les temps et de tous les pays*. Paris: Robert Laffont, pp. 7289-7292.

Made in the USA
Las Vegas, NV
21 July 2022

51893969R00017